MW00652593

Published by RXR Press

ISBN: 979-8-9895590-0-8

Illustrated by Marina Lina

To contact the authors about speaking or bulk orders of this book, visit www.stayforevergold.com

Printed in Canada

STAY GOLDEN, GIRLS

Chapters

Friendship is the New Marriage

Hi Girlfriends!!!

We're Rachel and Rachel and we met when we were 18, in college, and when the future was wide open. Degrees, parties, and boys were top of mind and probably not in that order.

We've now been friends for over three decades and supported each other through all of the ups and downs of marriage(s), children, and careers. We find ourselves in the cycle of life that also includes support after losing a parent.

While incredibly lucky to both be in happy marriages, we marvel more and more about how much we need and love our girl/female/women friends and cherish our times together. We've spent more time laughing our asses off than not, but as we grow older, we see how much value these same relationships mean in times of difficulty. Some friendships, maybe the best ones, see both extremes; life-saving to life-enriching.

One of the main inspirations for writing this book was an article we read about a group of seven girlfriends in China who bought an uninhabitable mansion to fix up and live in during their retirement years. We were so delighted to learn about how they put this real-life "Golden Girls" dream into action by pooling their resources and investing in their futures together. We have so much fun talking about living together one day, each of us contributing and bringing our strong suits to the table.

"I want to grow old with you" used to be reserved for romantic relationships, but not anymore. A proposal of a life spent together now includes our friends, not just lovers. After marriage becomes a legal commitment and the responsibilities of life settle in, a spouse may feel less like the dream supporter they once were during the courting period, a completely natural progression. Girlfriends retain the ability to let us shine and to dream while still holding us accountable on a different level. We want to make them proud, not because we are obligated to, but because we are inspired to.

Do you have a friend you're pretty sure is your soulmate but in a friend way?

Unlike the love for our children or our pets, friendships are not necessarily unconditional. Many women grew up socialized to think their marriages would be romantic, unconditional, and pure. Friends have the ability to wound and hurt the way

significant others do, but there's something about a modern-day friendship feeling closer to the concept of unconditional love than a modern-day marriage. Maybe because it's more about want than need or because our significant others know how to push our buttons. Or maybe it's because the grind of daily life allows us to take things out on the person who can't easily, physically walk out. It's a fact, the number one suspect in every murder case is the spouse (wink, wink, not the best friend!).

As we grow older, our friendships become even more important. A romantic relationship isn't the only planet around which we have to orbit. While marriage needs and deserves hard work, somehow the seeds of love planted between friends consistently grow with ease.

"Men, they come and go. They always will. Hopefully, they stay. But it's the girl that's sitting next to you that's going to get you through everything."

– Goldie Hawn

"Female friendship has been the bedrock of women's lives for as long as there have been women."

– Rebecca Traister

"Some people arrive and make such a beautiful impact on your life. You can barely remember what life was like without them."

– Anna Taylor

"Maybe we could be each other's soul mates. Then we could let men be just these great, nice guys to have fun with."

– Charlotte York, *Sex and the City*

The Best Medicine
Friendship is Therapy

Here's the best news!!! Our friends make us happier and healthier, and those benefits remain over our lifetimes. Friendships can be predictive of our day-to-day happiness and an indicator of how long we'll live, even more so than spousal and family relationships. Evidence shows when women feel emotionally close to other women, their bodies produce more progesterone, boosting mood and alleviating stress.

There's an ease of communication between friends, accounting for how therapeutic it feels to talk things out with them. To put it simply, friendship is therapy! We can express ourselves without fear. We connect, laugh, and maybe even have a cathartic cry. Friends support our emotional growth and healing by simply validating our emotions on one subject or another. They help us to be in the "moment" where we are more likely to experience peace and vitality, something that gets increasingly more challenging in daily life.

Would you believe loneliness is more dangerous than smoking 15 cigarettes a day? It's true. According to an advisory by the U.S. Surgeon General, loneliness is associated with a greater risk of cardiovascular disease, dementia, stroke, depression, and anxiety, and it increases the risk of premature death by approximately 26%. Our need to be a part of a community is not strange or unusual. We're hardwired to connect because being part of a community is not just nice, it's necessary for our survival. So what's the antidote to loneliness? Yep, you guessed it – friendship!

Support from loving relationships with women has proven to not only enrich our lives but also extend them. The London School of Economics found married men live longer than unmarried men, but the same benefits don't apply to married women! Maybe it's an added layer of maternal instinct or a desire to lovingly caretake, but let's just say, we can come to our own conclusions about the increased benefits of having devoted women looking out for us, and us for them.

We girlfriends have known all along what Harvard Medical School learned from the longest-running study in history, 75 years and counting, looking for predictors of healthy aging. Men, starting from their teens through their eighties, were interviewed every two years to gather information about their mental and physical health, career enjoyment, retirement experience, and marital quality. Across the board, the results found that the warmth of relationships has the greatest positive impact on one's life satisfaction, translating to happiness and fulfillment. Relationships have traditionally been where men falter, given that they've been socialized to prioritize success in other areas. Another reason women typically live longer than men, perhaps? What we do know is friendship is exactly what the doctor ordered!

"Thank you for always being there for me
and for the therapy I don't have to pay for."

– Anonymous

"Friendship is a wildly underrated
medication."

– Anna Deavere Smith

"Friends are medicine for a wounded heart,
and vitamins for a hopeful soul."

– Steve Maraboli

Trust (non) Issues

A true friend tells us that we look beautiful because that's the way they see us, even if we got no sleep, are totally hung over, or our makeup is running down our faces. That same true friend will also tell us, "Actually, they're just not that into you." We need real friends in our inner circles who challenge us to own our sh*% and tell us the truth, just as much as we need them to inspire us to shine. If we're lucky, they are one and the same. True friends are hard to come by and impossible to replace.

In life, sincere honesty is at a premium. When we feel comfortable enough to say hard things to our friends and safe enough to hear them said back to us, rest assured our friendships have reached a deeper level of authenticity. Who else but a true friend can we FaceTime from the dressing room of our favorite stores for an honest opinion? Our girlfriends may not always agree with us or share our views, but they want us to know the truth.

"Being honest may not get you a lot of friends but it'll always get you the right ones."

– John Lennon

"Look like a Bedazzler threw up on that thing... donate it to the My Little Pony Motorcycle Club."

– From the movie *Girls Trip*

"A best friend is someone who tells you the truth even when you don't want to hear it."

– Anonymous

Hopelessly Devoted to You

Perhaps the most prized quality of any friendship is loyalty. Loyal friends will always have our backs BEHIND our backs. They accept us with all our flaws, usually making light of them to help lighten us up. A loyal friend will give their time and energy from a seemingly bottomless well of love, where a payback is never expected and scores need not be kept.

One of the most challenging and gratifying things in life is accepting the mirror our friends reflect back at us. We all experience moments of doubt and weakness, when we may want to judge others, even our best friends. Often that weakness stems from our own disappointment or regret. But sometimes these moments come from frustration with our friends' decisions and choices. When we love someone, we don't want to see them f**k up and experience difficulty. Our loyalty inspires the honesty needed to help guide – but sometimes we just need to know when to shut up and offer a hand to hold.

"It's an insane world but in it, there is one sanity, the loyalty of old friends"

– Stephen Boyd

"Uteruses before duderuses. Ovaries before brovaries."

– From Leslie Knope, *Parks and Recreation*

"True friends aren't the ones who make your problems disappear. They are the ones who won't disappear when you're facing problems."

– Unknown

"Lots of people want to ride in the limo with you—what you want is someone who will take the bus with you when the limo breaks down."

– Oprah Winfrey

Life in the Laugh Lane

There is almost nothing better than having fun with a friend. Whether laughing, talking, sharing, or hanging out, it doesn't matter. Celebrating huge milestones or literally doing nothing, friends know how to have fun in any circumstance anywhere, any time.

Fun between friends can happen in the most unlikely places. It could be the ER waiting room when your friend has been bucked off a mechanical bull and split open her chin or at the dry cleaner when the planned outfit bombs and our most reliable dress is the only savior. And they don't write songs about meeting in the ladies' room for nothing! Getting ready together beforehand is often more fun than the actual event. We may even be dressing up with each other, for each other.

We can always rely on a true friend to lighten up and boost our mood, sometimes with a wildly inappropriate comment or gesture. When laughter turns to hysterics, we get an added ab workout. It's a win-win. When hysterics turn to peeing a little, we know our friend is a keeper.

"No matter what happens, I'm glad I came with you."

– From *Thelma & Louise*

"When you're in jail, a good friend will be trying to bail you out. A best friend will be in the cell next to you saying, 'Damn, that was fun."

– Groucho Marx

"If you fall I will pick you up. But only after
I stop laughing."

– Anonymous

"When I say 'Jump,' you say, 'On who?!'"

– Blanche, *The Golden Girls*

Bra Support

(Instead of Bro, Get It?)

The best part of any team is the camaraderie and how team-work makes the dream work! Girls' teams hold space for individual and group success. Friends are each other's best cheerleaders, whether we're out in front of the pack or especially when we're in the back and in need of encouragement.

It's a proven fact that when test audiences are recruited to watch films and television shows, the audience approval dial gets turned up the highest when a group of characters works together and comes out on top. Troop spirit is contagious, and with any squad, the louder and more in sync, the better and stronger the crew.

When we hold each other up, we happily encourage each oth-er's successes. After all, a rising tide lifts all boats, and lighting paths for others brightens our paths as well. Girls who are en-couraged at a young age to support one another create com-munity. This girl power transitions into even fiercer female superpowers. Seeing women take on roles we haven't seen in the past and killing it, especially with the reinforcement of other women, raises the bar and makes cracks in the glass ceiling. It's all the sweeter because we do it together.

Cheering on a friend and supporting a dream is joyful and inspiring. We find strength from a friend who is there to encourage us to test new waters. While we may not always say the exact/perfect/right thing at precisely the right time, encouragement comes naturally between women.

Our pandemic friendships proved this like no other time before, helping us get through loneliness, isolation, and fear of so much uncertainty. Our friendships were there to smooth out the rough patches and our phone calls, Zoom cocktail hours, and text chains became our lifelines. Even a few kind, funny, or loving words kept our emotional connection when physical distance for safety kept us apart. How sweet it was when we were able to once again embrace.

"Find a group of people who challenge and inspire you; spend a lot of time with them, and it will change your life."

– Amy Poehler

"There is no limit to what we, as women, can accomplish."

– Michelle Obama

"Abandon the cultural myth that all female friendships must be b*tchy, toxic, or competitive. This myth is like heels and purses - pretty but designed to SLOW women down."

– Roxane Gay

"A friend is one who overlooks your broken fence and admires the flowers in your garden"

– Unknown

"Some people go to priests; others to poetry. I go to my friends."

– Virginia Woolf

"Never let your friends get lonely... keep disturbing them."

– Anonymous

"It's the friends you can call up at 4 a.m. that matter."

– Marlene Dietrich

"Good friends don't let you do stupid things alone."

– Ain Eineziz

"I have learned that friendship isn't about who you've known the longest, it's about who came and never left your side."

– Yolanda Hadid

Mother Frienders

To have a mother or a daughter, biological or not, who is your friend, is the cherry on the sundae. It may take a while, but when we hit a certain age, our mother/daughter relationships hopefully shift into mutual admiration. What a blessing when we begin to take care of each other. It's inevitable, considering we may talk to our mother/daughter all the time and go to her for advice. We wear things out of her closet. We make her recipes. We may even look like her.

Our moms and mother figures know what we're thinking and what's right for us usually before we do, whether or not we can hear them when they say it. Mothers are the people who wish for our dreams to come true no matter how far the reach. It's why we as mothers encourage our daughters to spend time with their friends and to be kind and generous with them because we know their immense value. And when daughters become mothers, mothers and daughters get closer.

"A daughter is just a little girl who grows up to be your best friend."

– Anonymous

"The more a daughter knows about the details of her mother's life - without flinching or whining - the stronger the daughter."

– Anita Diamant

"First my mother, forever my friend."

– Unknown

"Mirror, mirror on the wall, I am my mother after all."

– As seen on a thrift store needlepoint pillow

Galentine's Day

Galentine's Day is celebrated on February 13th, the day before Valentine's Day. Amy Poehler's "Leslie Knope" first coined the term on the hit sitcom "Parks and Recreation" when she gathered a group of her close friends at a restaurant to enjoy breakfast. This new tradition that made it into the zeitgeist and popular culture is one to get excited about. When we read about Poehler's Galentine's celebration the same week our teen daughters were invited to a Galentine's sleepover, we knew something fresh and new was upon us with staying power. This pseudo-holiday began as a festivity just for the "gals," but Galentine's Day has transformed into an inclusive celebration in recent years, celebrated by everyone, whether married, in a relationship, or single. There's no monogamy needed.

Galentine's Day is, of course, like Valentine's Day but without expectation and pressure, a holiday dedicated to celebrating friendship in all its forms. How fun to shower our non-romantic soulmates with love. Regardless of whether or not we have a significant other and/or lover, our friends are there for us in ways our partners sometimes cannot be.

On this special festive holiday, we get to enjoy chocolate, tea, champagne, and flowers while toasting to being in love with friendship!

Galentine's Day looks like it's here to stay, like sound baths in oversized teepees, purse parties, book clubs, and the Tupperware parties of yesteryear.

"True friends are like diamonds- bright, beautiful, valuable, and always in style."

– Nicole Richie

"A friend is someone who makes it easy to believe in yourself."

– Heidi Wills

"Best Friends - They know how crazy you
are and still choose to be seen with you
in public."

– Unknown

"There is nothing better than a friend, unless it
is a friend with chocolate"

– Linda Grayson

Soul Sister Wives

A soul sister is a female friend not related by blood who shares a bond that transcends time, distance, and biology. When girlfriends become like family, we create a sisterhood, a bond so strong nothing can come between us. We share clothes, food, secrets... everything.

Of course, there are religions and cultures that go way beyond what we're talking about here, as dramatized in the hit television series, HBO's *Big Love*. Even a television show about actual sister wives, all sleeping with and bearing the same man's children, couldn't tamp down the connection between the female characters and audiences were won over.

If we're lucky enough to have a biological sister who is also a best friend, all the better. While there is no choice in who is born a sister, whether or not a sister becomes a friend is another story entirely. What could be better than having a built-in bestie in our house growing up, at family functions, and to weather parental life cycles? The inside jokes alone make this relationship priceless beyond compare.

"We're sisters; you're my family. What is you, is me. There's nothing that you could ever say to make me let go."

– Blair Waldorf, *Gossip Girl*

"I think a soulmate is a mate that helps you find your soul."

– Jay Shetty

"We made a deal ages ago. Men, babies, it doesn't matter…we're soul mates."

– Samantha Jones, *Sex and the City*

"There's one thing stronger than magic: sisterhood."

– Robin Benway

"When sisters stand shoulder to shoulder,
who stands a chance against us?"

– Pam Brown

"There is one friend in the life of each of us who
seems not a separate person, however dear and
beloved, but an expansion, an interpretation, of
one's self, the very meaning of one's soul."

– Edith Wharton

My Wine Glass is Half Full, My Coffee Cup Runneth Over

Nothing complements a glass of wine or goes with a cup of coffee quite like a friend by our side or across the table. Throw in some good music, a cheese board, or a warm croissant, and it's like hitting the jackpot. It's the best time to let the pressures of the day drift away as we savor the richness of whatever we're imbibing.

Friends can turn a cheer-up session into a downright celebration. We call it "comissibrating"- a cross between commiserating and celebrating. The fact we have a friend nearby during darker times is a reason to commemorate in and of itself. "Do you need to talk?" is a universal question that goes hand in hand with the cups we're holding.

Cultures all over the world have rituals involving women who raise glasses and mugs and "toast" their time together to celebrate big and small or nothing at all.

Check out how women partake across the globe:

Coffee

In Denmark, drinking coffee is a social activity, and the cafes are cozy hideaways where women relax during the day.

In Turkey, the ritual of drinking coffee together is known as "kahve." Women also exchange recipes and share advice on everything from cooking to relationships.

In Italy, coffee is a daily ritual especially important for women who gather in coffee shops to catch up. The most popular coffee drink in Italy is the cappuccino, usually consumed in the morning.

In Saudi Arabia, women often gather in their homes to drink coffee. Typically served in small cups, it's made with roasted coffee beans and cardamom. As they sip, they socialize, confide in one another, and share advice on family matters.

In the United States, women often meet in coffee shops to catch up on the latest news, share stories, and offer support to each other. The popularity of coffee shops has made

them a common meeting place for women of all ages and backgrounds.

Tea

In Britain, women have a long-standing tradition of taking tea in the afternoon with scones and other treats. Tea time is often seen as a way for women to connect and strengthen their friendships and where communication without interruption from the outside world is prized.

In Morocco, mint tea is a popular variety often shared between women during social gatherings, allowing them to bond over conversation and shared experiences.

In Japan, the tea ceremony, also known as "chanoyu," is a highly ritualized practice involving the preparation and serving of matcha green tea. Often performed by women and seen as a way to cultivate a sense of calm and inner peace, it strengthens friendships through a shared appreciation of beauty and simplicity. The tea ceremony is a symbol of harmony, respect, and tranquility. It is a way for women to connect with each other on a deeper level.

In India, "chai" is a staple beverage made with a blend of spices, including cardamom, cinnamon, and ginger. Whether shared between women during a social gathering or enjoyed throughout the day, it is savored and appreciated.

Booze

In Japan, there is a tradition of women drinking sake together in a group known as "nomikai." These gatherings often take place after work and serve as a way for women to socialize and build relationships outside of their professional responsibilities.

In Mexico, women often gather for a "mujeres noche," or "women's night," where they share food, drinks, and conversation. These gatherings are typically held in private homes and are seen as a way for women to support and celebrate one another.

In some African countries, such as Ghana and Uganda, there are traditional fermented drinks made from cassava or maize that are popular among women. These drinks are often brewed in small batches and shared among female friends as a way to bond and socialize.

Cheers to us, because ladies who coffee, tea, brunch, lunch, and cocktail together, stay together!

"The best wines are the ones we drink with friends."

– Unknown

"The best way to mend a broken heart is time and girlfriends."

– Gwyneth Paltrow

"As is the case of wines that improve with age, the older friendships ought to be the most delightful."

– Cicero

Ladies' Night/Girls' Trip

Whether it's a fabulous girls' trip, a girls' night out, or a girls' night in, we have more fun when we're together. When we get together as couples, we girls want to sit together because we have so much to catch up on, even if it's been thirty minutes since our last conversation. Don't tell our significant others, but sometimes we opt out of making plans as couples to make it a girlfriend gathering because of how much we enjoy each others' company. We don't want anyone else monopolizing our precious time together.

Often seen as a luxury, the girls' trip feels like something many women want to plan and save up for. It's no wonder they have become fodder for movies, television shows, books, and more. A road trip or a flight to a retreat is something to look forward to, so much so that we relish the countdown days til blast off. A key theme to the many text threads and calls leading up to a trip or an evening plan is the dress code. "What are we wearing?" is an essential logistical factor in deciding if the group shows up in sweats or heels. If budget restricts us to bonding time at home, sometimes no trip, club, or restaurant

compares to a DIY mask, delicious drink, and a favorite romantic comedy on the couch with our besties.

"What happens in... stays in..." was probably coined by a group
of women, absolutely on fire to be together on an escape/ad-
venture. It's not about misbehaving. Sure, releasing control
and letting go can lead to wild moments. But that infamous
phrase can also refer to the thoughts, emotions, and private
ideas shared between friends. And yes, they're not always fit
for public consumption back home.

"There is just no comparison between having a dinner date with a man and staying home playing canasta with the girls."

– Marilyn Monroe

"Go girl, seek happy nights to happy days"

– William Shakespeare

"You call it girls' night. I call it therapy."

– Unknown

New Friends

Throughout the different stages of our lives, new needs can and do arise. Sometimes a new girlfriend comes along at just the right moment. The friends we make in our adulthood are an important part of our vitality. Making a point to connect with new girlfriends, especially when they are from different backgrounds, enriches our lives in unexpected ways.

Making a new friend who is going through similar experiences can make all the difference for us to not feel alone. How wonderful for a new friend to welcome us into their world and for our eyes to be opened to new possibilities, music, food, ideas, and worlds. How incredible it is to invite a new friend in, enriching our hearts and souls by making space. Getting to know girlfriends and learning their stories is a beautiful gift of human connection.

New friends come in the form of work friends, workout friends, dog park friends, volunteering friends, and mommy friends. Or as our friend, Ali says when she mistakes celebrities on the street for people she knows in real life, "I know her from Mommy and Me" and we say, "No, that's

Eva Mendes." You can make a friend just about any place you find a like-minded woman. If you need a little help, there are over a dozen top-ranked friendship apps for meeting new girlfriends.

"Women's friendships are like a renewable source of power."

– Jane Fonda

"Yes'm, old friends is always best, 'less you can catch a new one that's fit to make an old one out of."

– Sarah Orne Jewett

"We are partners by fate. We become friends by choice."

– Jacquie McTaggart

"How beautiful is it to find someone who asks for nothing but your company?"

– Brigitte Nicole

"Since there is nothing so well worth having as friends, never lose a chance to make them."

– Francesco Gucciardini

Old Friends/Golden Girls

We have all heard the saying, "Make new friends but keep the old, one is silver the other gold." There is nothing quite like an old friend who knows us, maybe even better than we know ourselves. It goes without saying, the best old friend is the first to get the call with bad news and is the keeper of the secrets. She knows where all the bodies are buried, and threw away the shovel.

With old friends, the 'space-time continuum' is meaningless because it doesn't matter how much time has passed since the last visit. There is an unspoken secret language developed over time only we understand. It's like laughter lives inside us, simply waiting to come out, laughter shared between people who are in on the same joke, even when the joke is on us! Sensitivity and questioning go out the window and only the bedrock of connection and love are left.

Even when the world is at its worst and most ridiculous, an old friend can pull us up/cheer us up/crack us up with a look, pregnant pause, or one-liner that would make Carol Burnett or Tina Fey stand up and applaud.

*GOLDEN ˢᴴᴼᵂᴱᴿ GIRLS: When "old" friends are literally older...

Women growing old together understand each other on a deeper level. It gets to a point where words don't need to be expressed and we can communicate almost telepathically. We're kind of like an old married couple, but one who keeps laughing with the other. Forging passionate friendships outside of sexual activity or state-recognized monogamy, like "The Golden Girls" did, not only reverses the loneliness epidemic, it helps us women not just survive but thrive.

When we first started this book, we thought this section would simply be the necessary and reverent nod to the royalty of friendships: the besties, the soulmates, and the queens, the Golden Girls from the hit television show. Incidentally, we worked many hours together writing this book in the kitchen of a home once owned by Rue McClanahan who played "Blanche."

But about four months into researching this book and working on the essays, we had an experience we knew needed to be included in this section. We were on a girls' trip in Palm Springs, laughing our asses off while dancing to a cantina band and eating and drinking too much between dips in the jacuzzi. One night before dinner, Rachel was injured while helping the girls move something. With a

history of fainting, she knew she was going down and let us all know. After a shocking few long moments, she came to, seemingly fine, thank goodness. But soon she said, "I think I peed. I'm all wet." In a flash, the girls moved into action like a NASCAR pit crew, Rachel was cleaned up and given a new outfit, her wet clothes tossed in the washing machine. The jokes started flying that our feet were now firmly planted into the future of our life together as best and older friends, golden girlfriends for eternity.

On this thrilling ride of life with all its ups and downs, keep inspiring, supporting, and enjoying your treasured friends, and may you always STAY GOLDEN!

"We've been friends for so long, I can't remember which one of us is the bad influence."

– Unknown

"We are friends for life. When we're together the years fall away. Isn't that what matters? To have someone who can remember with you? To have someone who remembers how far you've come?"

– Judy Blume

"I've been having a good time, and there wasn't even a man in the room."

– Blanche, *The Golden Girls*

"My friends have made the story of my life. In a thousand ways, they have turned my limitations into beautiful privileges."

– Helen Keller

"Well, female friendships are fucking extraordinary."

– Keira Knightley

"A good friend knows your stories. A best friend helps you write them."

– Unknown

"A good friend will help you move, but a true friend will help you move a dead body."

– Jim Hayes

"I found out what the secret to life is: friends. Best friends."

– Ninny Threadgoode,
Fried Green Tomatoes

"We know now that no matter how far we traveled on our own separate paths… somehow we would always find our way back to each other."

– Lena and Bridget,
The Sisterhood of the Traveling Pants

"Make new friends, but keep the old. One is silver. The other is gold."

– Traditional *Girl Scouts* song

"Let's become little old ladies together-stay up late looking at old pictures, telling "remember when" stories, and laughing til our sides ache. Let's become eccentric together, the kind who take long walks, wear silly hats, and get away with acting outrageous in public places. And if anybody should ask how long we've been friends, we'll say, "Oh forever-since before you were even born!" Let's become little old ladies together because a friendship that's as special as ours can only grow better throughout the years."

– Unknown

Girls Inc.

Ten percent of the proceeds of this book go to Girls Inc., a non-profit focusing on the development of the whole girl. Girls Inc. was established in 1864 and is one of the longest continuously operating organizations offering girls-only programming encouraging girls to be "Strong, Smart, and Bold" through direct service and advocacy. Through Girls Inc., every girl learns to value herself, take risks, and discover and develop her inherent strengths. The combination of long-lasting mentoring relationships, a pro-girl environment, and evidence-based programming equips girls to navigate gender, economic, and social barriers, and grow up healthy, educated, and independent. Informed by girls and their families, Girls Inc. also advocates for legislation and policies to increase opportunities and rights for all girls. Together we can help our Girls to Stay Golden!

Acknowledgments

We want to give special thanks to Lawrence Azerrad, JB Bryans, Mary Rose Fernandez, Agata Filipczak, Mark Frazin, Darby Gidlow, Juli Bliss Kinrich, Marina Lina, Julie Neale, Todd Steinman, Camille Stidham, Terence Winter, and our girlfriends (special shoutout to our friend with FOMO), our mothers, daughters, and Rachel's son for inspiration.

"There are no words that can express my
thanks for you. If words could be hugs
I would send you pages."

– Unknown

About the Authors

Rachel Steinman is a writer, teacher, and mental health advocate. She hosts the *Dear Family, Podcast* with inspirational guests who have overcome mental health obstacles to thrive. She received her Masters in Education and teaching credentials from UCLA, has taught every elementary school grade, and has been the school's librarian. She is a lead presenter for NAMI (National Alliance on Mental Illness), going into middle and high schools to educate students, parents, and staff about warning signs while offering resources and hope. She's passionate about getting people to talk about mental health by replacing stigma, shame, and secrecy with love, compassion, and understanding.

Rachel Winter is a writer, director, and an Academy Award®-nominated producer for *Dallas Buyers Club*. Winter, along with LeBron James, produced James' biopic, *Shooting Stars*, released on Peacock in June 2023. Available now from IHeart Radio, Winter produced and directed the audio drama "Supreme: The Battle for Roe" starring Maya Hawke and William H. Macy. The nine-part series weaves together the incredible story of the young female lawyer who argued Roe V. Wade in front of the Supreme Court and the Justice who wrote the opinion. Winter made her directorial debut with *The Space Between*, starring Kelsey Grammer, for which they both received awards from various Film Festivals.